CW01022211

ISBN 978-0-9567348-0-8

Published by Sunshine Publishing
email: suesp@sky.com

Typesetting & Printing by

Clarkeprint Ltd
Waveney House
45-47 Stour Street
Ladywood
Birmingham B18 7AJ

In the

Twinkling of an eye

By
P E Spencer

Contents

EXPERT OF RENOWN

These poems are not written by an expert of renown
So eloquently using all the verbs, pronouns and nouns
But by a common man who's not designed it to a plan
And choreographed the lines, the whole
To pull your heart strings, wrench your soul

Lift you up or pull you down
The roller coaster of sounds
Of words with all that they purvey
Illuminating every day

But these poor tries of poem and rhyme
Have taken up not too much time,
For I will sit and write them down
 as I see them in my mind,
Not caring how I start each line
with I's and buts its such a crime

But I care not of such things,
if my lines will make you think
of things and times of long ago
when things were different and more slow
and again in modern times
with faster things and different rhymes.

I hope that you enjoy them all
and pass them on to everyone,
To make them smile or laugh or sigh
Of forgotten times and lighter skies.

MUNTJAC DEER

The little deer that came my way filled me with delight.
It trotted up the garden path and gave me quite a fright.
At first I thought it was a dog, and then again, a pig,
but it vanished in the shrubbery with just a little jig.

It had no horns or antlers and was so squat and small.
It looked unlike a pig or dog and not a deer at all.
It's eyes were black and shiny bright alert and fixed on me.
It's coat was brown or red or grey! Or did I really see?

It's body like a barrel didn't seem to fit it at all,
But still it seemed so dainty as it nimbly passed me by
And vanished in the shrubbery in the twinkling of an eye.

But now its gone the garden path seems empty and forlorn,
As if she never was here or was never born at all.
But now I can still see her in my mind's eye on the path,
Which makes me catch my breath again
and often smile and laugh.

CHILDREN QUESTION EVERYTHING

Where does the sun go in the night
What does it do when out of sight
Why does is stay away so long
And creep back up at morning's dawn

Why does the moon in pieces seem
Who puts it together with hidden seams
Where does it get its silvery glow
It seems so complicated, you know.

Why don't the clouds fall from the sky
And why do the trees grow up so high
Why is a baby born so small
And why are the mountains so very tall

Why do the swallows come back in spring
How do they find us, where have they been
Why does it rain when we play outside
And why do wild animals all run and hide

Why is the world full of questions for me
It's all so exhausting,
I'm off for my tea.

DAWN

Before the dawn grey shadows stand, silent and still across
The land,
As if in waiting to hear the call, heralding in another dawn.

The sky does lighten just a bit, beckoning the start of it,
Robin's quiet murmurs start the throng; on his favourite perch
He sings his song.

And not to be out-done, the wren starts up before the sun.
The nightingale, in this half light, fills the valley with delight.

His mellow charms seduce the day, which beckons to him, 'stay
Please stay'.

But look! Here comes a lighter sky, the woodlands echo to
The cry
Of many a hundred birds in song, singing this is where we
All belong.

The stormcock takes the highest branch, to sing his song and
May-be chance
To call a mate, who, with one glance,
Shall let him know his nest shall make, up in the elm tree by
The gate.

Blackbirds flit within the bush, and leaves fly by with such
A rush
His hen he thinks should be his own, but others want his
Lofty throne.

They chase and screech as feathers fly, and others cock their
Heads and sigh
For they hear not their own sweet songs, with the melee
Going on.

Then all at once the woods alive, a thousand birds set
To contrive
To out do their neighbours song; they sing much louder in
one throng

That radiates throughout the woods, and has done long before
Man stood
To stand in awe of such songs, illuminated by the throng
Of a hundred birds or more, reverberate you to the core.

And now the day is finally here, you stride away so full
Of cheer
To have witnessed such a throng. This must be just where
We belong.

RIVER FAIRY

I saw her today by the river,
Her dress of wild flowers and leaves,
Collecting wild garlic and singing
Of her love that is soon to be.
She caressed the May blossom while walking,
The scent drifting all through her hair,
Which was tousled
and fell around her shoulders
and onto her breasts that were fair

The song that she sang was so haunting,
Down the river it echoed and rang,
So softly, so sweetly enchanting
All creatures and even her man.

He heard her sweet calling from far away,
Stopped working and ran like the wind
To find his sweet love by the river,
Ever closer, but just around the bend.
He spied her now crossing the water
Floating blossom she gently did tread,
with mayflies adorning her hair now
and swallows around her they sped.

The otters now whistle to find her,
But on blossom she's long floated by,
To step off at the bridge by the willow,
Her love panting and breathless close by.
They kiss and embrace, it's enchanting
And float on the water like mist.
For fairies that live by the river
In daylight should never be kissed.

BOY AND THE BLACKSMITH

The boy took his horse to the blacksmith to shoe.
He's ne'er been before, he knows not what to do.
The blacksmith his forge spitting flames in the fire,
His hammer fast cleaning the flack from the iron.

With sparks flying everywhere and hot iron too,
It's not the best place if you're young or you're new.
The boy tethers his horse by the trough in the yard
To get a good drink while he looks inside.
He inches much closer towards the hot flames
As the sparks drew him in with his inquisitive brain.

'Stand clear young man', the blacksmith did say,
'Hot sparks they will fly in your clothes or your eyes
And the scale from the iron may fly through the air
And end up in your clothing or burning your hair'.

The boy took little notice of what he was told.
His excitement it grew as he got very bold.
With flack flying everywhere one piece did arrive
To lodge in his trousers and burn his backside.

He squealed out in agony and shot out the door
To quench his burnt bits in the trough by the horse.
The horse now alarmed by the screaming and splash
Pulled off its halter, down the lane it did dash.

With traces all flying he went like the wind
And was not seen for a fortnight, but that's not the end.
His backside now stinging he arose from the trough,
Hot flack from his trousers fell out with a plop

The blacksmith now striding and closing the gap
The boy saw Armageddon and so made a dash
Out through the yard and off down the lane
his backside still stinging from this awful pain.

One day next fortnight the horse wandered home,
Its traces in ribbons its shoes they're all gone.
His coat it was matted where he had rolled in the mud
and looked like a nightmare where he whinnied and stood.

The boy's now still paying for the damage that's done.
He now carefully listens to everyone
Whose advice it is given although sometimes stern
If you listen and follow it you'll very soon learn
That the trouble you cause when you take little heed
Could cost you a fortune and many more deeds.

CHICKENS

Chickens scratching in the yard, a great life and not too hard!
Each to their own within the flock, peck order kept by one old
cock
Who in the morning crows and calls; 'I am the boss, look out
you all!'

He leads them first to have a drink for breakfast, last night
corn he thinks.
And then they're off around the patch to cluck and crow and
have a scratch
Finding lots of things to eat beneath the leaves, they hunt and
seek.

After lunch the sun it shines while chickens sunbathe in one
line
Beside the wall's reflective heat they stretch out lazily to sleep.

But when a shadow comes to fall across the sky the cockerel
calls
With one great scowl he tells his fowls
'Look out , look out dangers about!'
As from the sky it often falls in darker shapes of owls and
hawks
And when its past they take no heed, off again they go to sleep.

The sun goes in and up they get, all clucking now they've had a
rest
Off towards the bonfire ash to settle in for a dust bath.

While these things are going on hens slip away one by one
Into the nest box full of hay to sit there quietly and lay.
With much clucking, they proclaim all celebrating with the
same
About the egg that's come to be, and how for someone's tea
may be.

The shadows grow much longer now, the farmer calls in all the cows.
Cockerel stands upon the fence, he beats his wings and throws his head.
His crowing brings back all his hens, he says "girls now it's time for bed".

So to roost they make their way, to sit and dream about the day,
And then tomorrow with the dawn the cockerel's crow will wake them all.

STICKY BITS OF PAPER

Sticky bits of paper all about my chin
She said you look a sight old Jack
Wherever have you been?

I said I had been shaving stubble two days old
The razor wasn't sharp enough
But I was feeling bold.

There was no hot water and very little soap
As I took a great big deep breath
And said a prayer of hope.

Well the razor it did half the job but I still lived in hope
As I shaved off half the stubble
And half my chin, I felt a dope.

So I took the old newspaper and tore off little bits
To stick them on my poor old chin
That was cut up to bits.

I know that I do look a sight but please remember this:
Thank the stars you're not a man
To end up in such a mess.

She said 'I'll kiss it better Jack so sidle over here'.
I guess that shaving's not too bad
Tonight I'll have a beer.

SOFTLY CAME THE NIGHT

The winter's night was still and calm,
It folds around you like two arms.
The darkness, soft as satin sheets,
To hide the secrets all night keeps.
Up in the tree the last to call
Cock pheasant shouts 'I've done it all'.
Off to bed he boldly goes
Around the branch tightly his toes.

And softly comes the night.

The owls start calling to and fro
Which way to come and where to go
Small birds hide in holly bush
Some startled cause a great big rush
To find a perch more safe and sound
But one flies out upon the ground.

The owl who's waited patiently
Says here's a sparrow just for tea.
On silent wings he glides on air
The sparrow sits there, unaware,
His vision cannot see his doom
In this velvet, secret gloom.

And softly comes the night.

The vixen calls to find her mate
She barks, then screams, he's not about.
This she'll keep up all night long
Until some food he'll bring along
And drop it at their chosen earth.
To start to play, both full of mirth,
Very soon within the spring
Cubs in the earth will make it ring,

With yelps and squeals and playful sounds
Emanating from the ground

And softly comes the night.

The rabbits by the score abound,
For fox is safely underground.
They feed and chase and play some more
And will do off and on till dawn.

And softly comes the night.

It's now mild and there's no frost.
The badgers search for worms,
Quartering around the ground
Where bugs and earthworms may abound.
They notice not the cows and sheep.
Should man arrive when he should sleep,
They scuttle off with gruff disdain
And wish on him that it would rain

And softly comes the night.

At half past two it's just that time
When night it gets much colder.
All that walks or flies or crawls
Except for those much bolder
Have crept away to rest awhile until the night is over.

And softly comes the night.

The dawn it finally appears with noises
That we all have heard.
One rabbit missing off the lawn
One sparrow silent from his song.

The field looks ploughed where badgers worked
To find the earthworms in the dirt

Cock pheasant in the morning sun
Struts and crows, 'I am the one'.
His feathers in such dazzling form
Complete this bright and dewy morn

And softly goes the night.

THE BALLOON

You may have a lot of troubles, my father said,
There is no need to huff and puff, it just gets in your head
And stops you doing other things which will please you more
Instead of screaming flat out on your face upon the floor.

He said, there is a better way and not to huff and puff
But when it gets you in this way you have to take a breath.
Imagine that your huff and puff is filling a balloon
Then let it go and watch it flying quickly round the room.

The noise it makes as it takes off will make you smile and
say,
I think I'll never worry anymore or anyway.
And now I am much happier, I smile and never care
About things that don't matter or just get in my hair.

My life is so much happier and I am never sad
But I owe it all to that balloon and my special dad.

OUTSIDE

Outside is where I need to be, over the fields and woods I'm free
To stay out late till two or three. The night owl's calling sets me free

To travel on until the dawn not considering to yawn
Or feel tired and sleep to take over the moor must morning make

The quiet night and solitude is startled by the morning mood.
The wind gets up, not just a sigh, a multitude of clouds rush by.

While walking through the village, though it's early, 'late for me'
No one stirs about, there no one in the world to see.

The dogs that snap upon your heels are sound and fast asleep
The village like a postcard sitting clean and bright and neat.

Walking through the garden gate and breakfast tea and last nights cake
To reflect on my night's work and watch the village shake and stir.

As they walk by in ones and twos they talk together 'what does he do?'
Sits in his garden late in the day,
Where does he work how does he earn his pay?
I smile and lay down on the lawn, the dog close by his ears all torn
from thorns where he had plucked for me a rabbit for this evening's meal.

VICTORY AND GLORY

They joined up not for victory but to learn a trade to set them free
From poverty and grime of a downtrodden town
For there was no talk of war wherever could it be!!
And so they joined the forces to learn a trade and set them free.

Alas as with all better plans, we all do fail to see
There often is a down side, and the war it was to be.
The trade I'd learned when I joined up was mixed in with the rest
Of very much hard training just to make us all the best

But all the training in the world could not prepare us for
'Their' victory or glory but for us just hell and war.
I will not talk about it. Leave it in the field they say
And march back through your home town as if you're on parade

They all come out to welcome you as heroes and the brave
But they never see the real men who have forever changed.
Their families see it daily as more quiet times they need
To reconcile just what they've done they work with faster speed

Nightmares while they are sleeping and in their thoughts Today
Of friend and comrades they have lost, and left along the way.

They wonder what it's all about as they try to get a job
And are told you need re-training, it's a shame you were
demobbed.

Well, its easy for them to say, just sit a few exams
And get certificated and then you'll soon feel grand.
But they don't have to sit there filling in those questionnaires
While your mind is dodging bullets whistling through the air

But as they've said it many times no matter how you feel
"what goes on in the field stays in the field".

It now seems so unreal.

THE FEATHER

A feather floats down from the sky
Catches the wind catches my eye,
Floats like a boat upon the sea,
Sails ever closer to me.

The breeze it rises with a sigh
And lifts the feather way up high,
To fall again in swirls and curls
Just like a boat with sails unfurled.

I run and jump and try to catch
The little feather in my hand.
Its quill so hard, the down so fine,
The feathers painted with design.

So colourful and complete,
It makes the day a real treat.

WOODLAND FAIRY

No dress she had with sequins bright, the dance was close that
very night.
She pulled the cobwebs pearled with dew to decorate the dress
she knew.
With spiders silk she nimbly sewed this length of pearls.
Around she goes
With hoar frost on some frozen leaves to decorate her tiny
sleeves.

And holly berries bright and red upon this silken spider's
thread
A necklace made, so neat that shone so very bright, just like
the sun.
Some icicles she went and found around the hem she tightly
bound.
And as she moved and danced with glee a peel of tiny bells set
free.

Now ready for the dance she went thru field and woodland to
the glade
Where fairies, pixies, gnomes and elves were celebrating
winter's end.
About the fire they danced and laughed, the flames danced too
within this hearth,
Shafts of light and flickering hues illuminating all they do.

She gazed upon this ring so bright, flames lit the circles
dancing light
Slipping in where none could see, half in the light and shadows
be
To dance around and join the rest, each one wants to be the
best.

As she moves from dark to bright, her dress reflecting the
firelight,

Like rare gem stones light ensues, casting out so many hues
Icicles around the hem made music like sleigh bells
and caused the crowd of pixies to stop dancing with the elves.

They stood and stared in disbelief at this angel made of frost
and leaves,
With icicles and frozen dew dancing to the pipers tune.
And as she danced without a care faint woodland breeze lifted
her there
Then let her down upon the grass to jump and twirl within the
dance.

With moonlight shining through her hair making out a
halo there,
She flits about through dark and light now no-one dancing, its
all quiet
The pipers stopped and they're all still she dances on her mind
so full
But all at once she stops and sees they are all now gazing, she
does freeze.

Then like the smoke from off the fire she's gone within
the trees.
They think, well did they see her, or was it just a dream,
A figment of their imagination? They stare into the wood in
disbelief
But far off in the distance they know that she was real from
the sound of tinkling icicles
like a thousand tiny bells, they peel.

LIQUID SUNSHINE

Raindrops come in many ways from downpours or in misty haze
Before the rain the songbirds sing, causing the woodlands merry ring.

Sometimes like stair rods it will pour on tin roofs like thunder roar
Rattling the beams inside will even make the spider's hide.

Chickens scamper to the barn and ducks just sit 'there is no harm'.
Cows, they stand beneath the trees with raindrops falling from the leaves.
They chew their cud and take no care for when it stops they'll still be there.

Some early morns or misty nights the rain takes on a different guise.
It turns to mist, its droplets fine soak through your coat in double time.

Throughout the day with sunshine bright rain takes on a special sight
It causes rainbows bright and bold with colours that gently unfold.

Raindrops mean so much to us because they give us life.
They wash away the daily grime and with it all our strife.

So when it rains don't moan and mind
just say the rain's liquid sunshine.

BOOKS

If you're just sitting there with something in your head
You would rather not think of or often times just dread

Don't kick off your shoes and switch on the old box
To distract yourself from everything and the daily knocks

But pick up a book, a good story to find
or one full of verse and some simple rhymes.

You'll forget all your troubles in double quick time
as you read on intently of stories and rhymes.

Your cares they won't matter what ever's been done,
as you simply enjoy both the story and fun.

And, afterwards, feeling alive and refreshed
You will have learned what some others
could never have guessed.

So do something with it, in your everyday life,
To help many others with their everyday strife.

Don't forget what I tell you for when you next hear
of the problems surrounding someone or some dear

Remember to tell them their troubles will clear
If they pick up a book full of stories and cheer.

THE OLD MAN

I saw him each day as I briskly walked by
To just say hello or a wink of the eye
Or occasionally stop to sit down for a chat
Of his life long ago or this and that

He seemed always to be there, Forever it seemed
Watching the world or just, Seeming to dream.
Others would nod as they walked on by
Without hesitating or stopping – they're shy!

But when I was with him I learned of his past,
His family and friends now gone or just lost.
We would talk about flowers and vegetables too
How he would grow them and what he would do.

Even his love life which came as a surprise
He told me his secrets and twinkled his eyes.

One day while passing, he was gone from his chair
While neighbours stood talking about his demise,
Their eyes fixed intently on his vegetable prize.
For none of them knew him or what he had been
His long life now ended and only a dream.

I think of him often sitting there in his chair
His mind full of wisdom with no one to share
But I learned a lot from him just stopping there
and I hope that in heaven friends welcome him there.

And give him the comfort he's missed all these years
And swap their old stories and dry his old tears

PHONE BILL

The post arrived just yesterday and with it came the bill
Amongst the other letters it was a bitter pill.

But what a shock to see the price; you would have thought me grand
To have so many friends to call, all throughout the land.

They all have jobs much grander and are paid much more than me
But this phone bill was enormous so I had to look and see
To see just who I had to call and who had called me.

Luckily the bill was itemised and I did not once surmise
The evidence was clear to see on the bill before my eyes.

The hours I spent just listening to their whines and moans
I could have earned a fortune even selling rag and bones.

I realised this had to stop and left the phone alone
And didn't try to call them on my dog and bone.

The weeks went by so silently and I got so much done
I started just to smile again and have a lot of fun.

For all the time just listening to their petty moans
I didn't think or realise their moans were just their own.

I often took them on myself you would think I was a shrink
To help them all would seem my goal until I stopped to think.

They had never tried to call over the weeks that fast flew by
So I guess I never needed them to call or just say Hi.

The cash I saved well! I could spend on myself or on my home
And never will have such a bill from that expensive phone.

YESTERDAY

Late for breakfast
Late for tea
Late for dinner
on his knee
Late for school
and late for home
Late for play
and late by phone
Late for parties
Late for friends
Late for haircuts
more split ends
Late for planes
and late for trains
Late for shelter
in the rain
Late for church
his wedding too
Late for all he has to do

So his friends re-named him today
and now they call him

"Yesterday"

THEY

I lay there just wondering a long time after tea
Of what they said or hadn't said and how they'd done for me.
I was waiting for the hiding that was sure to come
When my father heard the story of what I'd never done.

My voice was never listened to well it had never been
For they believed the others that would always lie or scheme.
The others wished that they were me, I knew it all along.
They envied all my stories and the lyrics of my songs.

For they had been just nowhere through the day or sang along
The woodland paths and field ways. The places I belong.
They had not seen the simplest things or heard the linnet song
Which whistled on the way back home and practised all night
long.

I think it drove them crazy hearing such a pretty song
and they wondered where I'd heard it but they wouldn't come
along.
Instead they listen to my tales about what I had done
and turned it all around again for just a bit of fun.

But when I heard it the next day it sounded not the same
and got me into trouble with a multitude of blame.
Well I could take my medicine, something they could not
and afterwards be sent to bed with somewhere feeling hot.

Well I could not sit still for long and so I'd go alone
Down the drainpipe from the bathroom to the only friends I'd
known.
Sitting within the woodland in the dark night all alone.

I would hear a million noises squeaks and screeches and some
moans
For what I couldn't see, I would picture in my mind,
a host of many animals which were much more than kind.
For they will never realise the things that they have missed,
The early morning sunrise and the soaking wet with mist

To know you have to leave here and walk a long way back,
Not relishing the ultimate, that one almighty whack
Which will be the start of it, a thunderstorm of pain
But I know they will never stop me, I'll just do it all again.

To them it was a battle to be won at any cost.
To me it was the freedom so that I could just get lost,
Get lost among the woodlands, the fields and any where
Where humans didn't like to go or often wouldn't dare

For then I'd go and see my friends who wouldn't lie an' scheme
And listen to the bird songs as if like in a dream,
A dream where everything was nice and happy as can be
But I am only ten years old and no one hears me

PLANS INSIDE YOUR HEAD

We all make plans precisely and store them in our heads
Making promises to finish them and tie up all loose ends.

But for most of us the plans we keep are only just a dream
Though they can become reality if you only get more keen.

So pick one plan, the smallest and easiest to complete
Set your alarm one hour in front to get early on your feet.

You won't feel like breakfast or morning TV, so you'll think!
Because that extra hour will have put you out of sync.

It will give you time to organise the things you have to do
and eventually complete the plans that others never knew.

One hour a day is all you need, seven it makes within the week.
One whole day you have just made the week was seven and
now its eight.

Over the weeks and year to come so many things you will have
done.
You will forget the old TV as plans you thought just couldn't be
Materialise before your eyes, you wake one morning full of
surprise.

The plans you had inside your head and looked on them as
something dead
Have with one hour a day arrived to fruition, now alive.

THE HUNT

Four fox cubs one day hatched a plan, never to be caught
by man.
Instead they planned when they grew up, they'd teach
the hounds
that wily cubs, would run them round, confuse the scent
and leave them floundering with intent.

The day it came, the hunt was on, the spectacle within
the throng
of horses, hounds and huntsmen all,
dressed to the nines just like a ball.

The horn did sound and they're away,
to draw the thicket, wood and kale
Eventually they found, by a very noble hound,
from old stock, his lineage rare, he cost a fortune but he
was there.

His cry went up the others joined in music of sheer joy.
Their music echoed through the dale
Across the stubble, up to the kale.
Reynard came out of the other side. Off to the big wood he
to hide
With no real pace, effortless and smooth
He galloped up the ploughman's groove.

The hounds they feathered here and there.
To find the scent that wasn't there.
But all at once the cry was there. It was fox and not a hare
Now in full cry they closed the gap.
Old Reynard's not a happy chap
But in the wood he sees his pal, Old Todd, he knew him
very well

As arranged Todd set off, to lead the hounds up to the croft
While Reynard has his well earned rest.
The hounds are still so full of zest
They close on Todd with sudden ease.
He miscalculated his last feed,
Eating his fill may pay the price
Unless the drain where vixen lays can be reached
so very soon never will he see tonight's moon
At the drain the vixen waits.
She's heard the hounds down by the gate.
Todd falls into the drain and groans,
Get going quick or we'll be toast.

Off she goes and cuts the scent,
The hounds arrive and think Todd went
Away the hillside, down she goes fresh as a daisy on
nimble toes.

The hounds check briefly at this spot
Scenting the vixen they move off.
The valley fills with hounds' music.
Vixen thinks she should be quick
To head up back to the big wood
Where at the gate her brother stood
He sees the hounds are mighty fit,
They've run ten miles and very quick
Though I can see they are starting to flag,
Tonight I won't be in the bag.

The sky is paling, daylight fades, hounds in kale are
called away
The huntsman smiles, what a great day, home we go,
We're on our way.

Fox looks out from in the bales,
Our cubs next year shall have some tales
As we recount our escapades
And their best run did history make.

COME TO ME

I tried to write a poem
But the words they would not rhyme
I tried to write some music
But the tune it wouldn't chime.

I tried to paint a swallow
Flying through the sky
Eventually I gave up,
With one enormous sigh.

Instead I sat there silently,
Cloaked in the summer green,
And watched the swallows in the sky
And heard their summer twittering cry

The sound far off church bells
And the calling of the cows
The whisper of the summer corn
and skylarks high soon after dawn.

And wondered why I bothered
To emulate these special things.
When all I had to do,
Was sit silently
And let them come to me.

EYES

I once saw a lady so bright and so fair.
It wasn't her smile and it wasn't her hair
But something about her.
I didn't look twice
For they were magnetic,
Her beautiful eyes.

For therein was wonder
And promises too.
They flashed like the sun
Were they green, were they blue?

They would melt into tenderness
Then with one glance
Could tell you she loved you
Or you have no chance.

One eyebrow now lifted
Would question it all,
While lifting you up
and then letting you fall.

With one sideways glance,
As she walks away,
She could say come tomorrow
Or you're yesterday.

You would never notice her clothes
Or her hair.
Her complexion so perfect
With no make-up there

For when you saw her
You look with surprise
As she flashes like lightening
those beautiful eyes.

GRANDAD

'Come here young man', the old man said,
'You look like you've just got out of bed'.
'He's been out all night', my ma replied.
The old man's eyebrows hit the sky,
'Come here and tell me what you've done'
And so I sat there and began:

I told my grandad where I'd been
And what I'd done and what I'd seen.
The tale I told took such a time,
I wore him out and then the chime
Of teaspoon falling on the tray
With biscuits and a cup of tea
My grandad sighed and looked real stern.

'I think young man you'll have to learn,
to do things right and obey or
I'll clatter your backside with this tray'.

'Go out and play with other boys
Try sport and books and other toys
To tire you out so you will sleep
and not the night owls company keep'.

'Your conversation will then expand and widen like the sky
And every sentence will not start with that inevitable "I".
So I think we'll call you "Mr I", it suits you very well,
For all we've heard is 'I've done this and I've done that as well'.

And so it stuck until the end he called me "Mr I".
I often used to hate the name but, as the years went by,
I came to realise this name he had given me was mine
For no-one else had got a name like my "Mr I".

And I was proud of what I'd got and never felt alone
For in my conversations whenever I said 'I'
I'd remember my grandad and the day he called me "Mr I".

Twinkling in my eye

I remember there was nothing,
Just the twinkling in my eyes,
Though yet your not existing
You would follow me close by
I felt your spirit with me,
Even when I was a child.
I always knew that you were there.
You always made me smile

You were in the space it often seemed
Not here not there but in-between.
Was it a sound or smallest sigh
Or shadows just outside my eye?
Was that you or are you real?
Sometimes I know not how I feel.

While laying still my mind would try
Or walking softly in the night
To see what you would be or might
But after all there was no sight.
Instead I knew that you were there
And that one day we'd come to share
A space in time upon this earth
To be filled with such great mirth.

I know exactly when you came
Into existence with the flame.
The day, the time, the hour, the whole
Embellishing my very soul.
The wait it seemed would never
end as I waited on this special friend.

THE OLD DOG

The Old Dog came in from the rain he thought he would retire
he shook his wet coat – briskly and nearly put out the fire.

The fire protested vigorously and hissed and spat the flames
the old dog lay down by it and groaned with his old pains.

He fell into a deep sleep and dreamt he was so young
chasing the sheep over the hill all the way to kingdom come.

His legs they start to tremble while galloping in sleep
to get ahead of that mad flock and bring them back to keep.

With eyelids flickering wildly as the sparks shot out the fire
to round up all the sheep was his only desire.

Although his coat was singeing he never missed a beat
as he chased the cows down highways and turned them in the
street.

His lips curled with a grimace and a throaty growl
emanated from him as he gave a muffled howl.

For whatever he was witnessing while he was fast asleep
was gone in an instance as he jumped up on his feet.

His coat it smelled so awful singeing hair and lots of smoke
Which sent the old dog dashing around the kitchen full of hope

That he could find the doorway and dive into the pond
to quench his burning tail of which he was so fond.

He moved so fast like lightening, we never saw such speed
for he could win the Grand National and beat most any steed.

We chased him around the kitchen with buckets in our hands
to quench the fire from off his tail and maybe save a strand.

Well each time that he passed us we would launch out half a
pail
which soaked around most everything but never reached his
tail.

With pots and pans and cutlery flying everywhere
and hats and coats asunder over an upturned chair.

Eventually he found the door as agile as a cat
He vaulted the table with one leap and also cleared the mat.

Outside he sped down to the pond his tail in there to soak.
Eventually when he returned he thought it not a joke

He looked at us as if we'd been conspirators to the scheme
and after that when he retired no longer lay down by the fire

But lay beneath the table where, he snarled and growled
and chased the hares and if he got too boisterous
while we sat down to eat we would all kick off our shoes
and tickle him with our feet.

AFRICA

While driving down the motorway I suddenly came to see
Galloping straight towards me was I sight I shouldn't see.
It seems a herd of wildebeest was on the motorway
But it was only motor cars speeding along their way.

They reminded me of Africa with a herd some thousand strong
Migrating to fresh pastures while others tagged along.
Sports cars were the cheetahs fast and sleek, then gone
With others lagging far behind and mingling with the throng.

Hot hatches were hyenas, lots of noise, bad manners too,
Never mind old Africa, it's more like London Zoo.
Juggernauts like elephants, long and large and slow,
Travelling in a convoy, with their special place to go.

Crane lorries like giraffes, their gait purposeful and sedate,
Though not so many of them, never wanting to be late.
With noise and smoke and horns galore
You may even hear the lions roar,
As drivers curse and strain their nerves
When cutting up causes a swerve.

The vultures waiting by the side rescue lorries never hide,
Without them now we would be lost,
So don't break down at any cost.
Now I arrive at journey's end the hectic traffic seems like friends
Not to un-like African plains, they seem no longer such a pain.

THE HOUSE

They promise to help, so they say,
but I'm still waiting here every day.
I continue to wait but they're not at the gate
and not even themselves on the way.
They say that they'd come very soon
but you'd think that I lived on the moon.
It's taken so long I don't think I'll hang on.
They won't come anyway in the gloom.

The day that they said they'd arrive, it
Made me feel so alive.
But by noon it was plain
That they failed yet again
To remember or even arrive.

The things that we all should have done
Have lingered and lingered on.
Asked why they never came
They failed to explain.
Or that something came up or I simply forgot
Was all that I heard in vain.

So I'll do what's to do by myself.
It will take so much longer, it's hell.
I'll push and strain and then do it again,
Though my bones they do ache
And my muscles they quake.
I'm left bleeding, breathless and sore,
Because when I'm done
I won't need anyone
To come smiling and knock at my door,

And to say, well done, look, we've all come
To see what a good job you've made.
I'll say thank you for the call and God bless you all
But don't bother to call round again.

HEAVEN

Some say heaven is pure chocolate for breakfast and for tea.

Some say it is the chance to shop until you're on your knees.
Some say it is a holiday in some exotic place
With half a pint of sunscreen poured upon your face.

Some say it is a child's laugh, a giggle, squeal or burp,
That makes you think that heaven is down upon this earth.

For me the sight of heaven is the smile upon your face,
The love that's in your eyes and the touch of your embrace.

To know that you are always, here upon this earth
and heaven's not so far away, when you're always near.

GOOD AT SOMETHING

We are all good at something. But I am not.
I never finish what I start and often just forget.
I start with such excitement, determined to complete
The tasks that should take just one day
Will take me many weeks.

I make up some excuses as I go from job to job
So that I don't get despondent while I try to earn a bob.
But I will do just anything to put obstacles in my way
And stop me finishing any job, not getting any pay.

I don't know why I do it; it just comes naturally,
As if what I see in my mind's eye
Should never come to be.
But now I am so good at it, whatever comes my way,
No matter how hard I try, I never finish on the day.

So now I work for other folk, working only half a day,
And at lunch time I rush off for another to make hay.
Now I am so successful with this better plan
That I'm earning quite a fortune,
And am now a richer man.

WHAT THE DARKNESS HIDES

The satin night enfolds me. Soft breezes caress my skin.
The stillness and the darkness keep you out, not let you in.
But if you listen carefully and keep very still
You may learn something about the night
That others never will.

You have to have much patience, it's really not a skill
To see and hear the things you want,
Will give you such a thrill.
For the creatures of the night can see far better and with ease
And any movement that you make will surely make them freeze.

Their gaze will fall upon you while their ears work overtime
To catch the slightest noise you make
And give them space and time.
Their nose will catch the slightest scent that drifts upon the breeze.
And mixes with the smell of grass and of many other trees.

So if you are to experience the things that darkness hides
First get the breeze into your face, and never walk, just glide.
You stand there quite patiently and you'll be surprised
At the things that happen, and what the darkness hides.

RECOLLECTIONS

Recollections of my early times,
sounds of the birds songs,
melodious chimes.

And the scent of box bushes
just after the rain
that you never forget and find
hard to explain.

The scent of fresh grass on the
newly mown lawn
and the nightingales song
in the dusk and the dawn.

This patch of grass was the
world that I knew
In the pram on the lawn
where I listened and grew.

THE JAY AND THE WIZARD

Sitting in the tree tops in the wood down by the stream
The Jay bird sat and sang his song so eloquently, all day long
The envy of all other birds, his song was great, maybe superb.

His feathers then were dowdy brown and he then had no
headdress crown.
All others passed him unseen, as if like in some sort of dream
And noticed not him sitting there in dowdy cloak on branches
bare.

So he went to find the wizard of the woods and hoped that he'd
be kind
and help him if he could
To make his feathers bright and shine astounding those that
came around
and maybe he would come to be noticed by all who passed him
by.

The wizard said this he could do but forfeit something dear to
you.
Anything, the Jay replied.
The wizard said just close your eyes and when you next do
open them
the envy off all others be with colours that have never been
in English woodland ever seen.

On opening his eyes he saw a cloak of feathers bright and bold
never before had he beheld the perfect cloak others would tell.

Into the treetops up he flew to sing out loud of what was new.
But try and sing just as he may, out came a croak and caw,
'dismayed'.

For the thing that they all envied was his special song,
They looked not at his dowdy cloak as they passed by within a
dream,
Who now in his special colours can do nothing more than
screech.

So be careful what you wish for while you're going through
your day
and make the best of what you have, don't end up like Mr Jay.

NURSES

Nurses dashing everywhere as busy as the bees
Answering the bells that call and managing with ease.

The jobs that come are varied and some impossible to do
But they manage every one of them with no time to find the loo.

Tea breaks now forgotten when emergencies arrive
To confound their expectations of a date with someone nice.

They battle on regardless with whatever should be done.
To save a soul from heaven, they do their best for everyone.

But when their shift has ended and they make it home
To catch a well earned rest and switch off the old phone

They find their shifts just started with washing and housework
They think to leave it till next week but they are never shirks.

So they go and set about it and soon it is all done
They collapse upon the sofa with some tea and Chelsea buns

So if you see a nurse having a cup of tea never think about her
That she is lazy

For she puts in more hours than are on the clock
And deserves a smile and thank you for this very well done job.

POETRY

If I could write some poetry that would make you smile,
To make you laugh and chuckle while your going many miles
To make you sigh with longing and cry out loud in bed,
'I don't believe he's written this, my goodness what he's said'

To make the tears run down your cheeks, your toes make
Circles in the sheets,
To make your eyes burn endlessly with such a blazing fire
And your heart be fit to bursting with a mountain of desire.

Alas I'm not a poet just a man who makes up rhymes,
So I guess I'll never write these things, maybe another time.
But I will write some poetry that will make you laugh and
smile,
As you travel life's old highways over many a mile.

HAUNTED WOOD

Tell me all about, my love, what's called the haunted wood.
I pass it oft in daylight, at night I never could.
It seems so bleak and desolate, so gaunt
And tall and dark. with no sound
Coming out of it, where demons must abound.

The tales they tell about it send shivers down my spine.
They say that it is haunted, due to an horrific crime.
A crime that was so long ago and evil with intent
But folk will go but only once,
Then at church they pitch their tent.

Well my love its plain to see the rumours
Told for those like thee
But fear them not because I know
The haunted wood's the place to go
For people far and wide won't go
Into the wood spring, summer or snow
But I go often day or night and fear not anything or fright.

Within the day birdsong abounds
Sunlight through branches swathes the ground
Bluebells and flowers of delicate hue
Carpet the floor, hidden well from view.

At night the moonlight filters down
And makes it easy to get around.
To travel quietly and see the secrets known only to me
So my love I'll take you there to stand or sit and quietly stare
At things that other folk do fear, you'll see it all so plain, so clear.

SO MAKE A CHANGE

When you're dissatisfied with all and everything you touch
does fall
To catch it seems just not to be, Another great catastrophe
If you feel bogged down with life your feet in mud, they're
stuck so tight,

Your energy so low -not even chocolate makes you go
Into the pantry for to see the biscuits, cakes and pastry
That will quell your feelings down and lift you up a little now
So if you want to make a change just look around and
rearrange

A chair or vase the TV too its the easiest thing to do
Or changes from your cornflakes to toast and marmalade
Or simply rearrange the clock to give you some more time.

These simple things just one of them will make a change
And amend
Some of the things within your life its patterns now changed
Will surprise.
For you will get so much more done and more energy will come
So you will find in a short time your life has changed
Through this short rhyme.

AUTUMN FAIRY

Born one early autumn morn of crickets calls and golden corn
No tears or cry from out they came but smiles of happiness
so plain.

Her eyes shone like the autumn sky with never sadness or
a sigh
But gentle laughter, smiles and words of encouragement,
not hurt

Her gentle ways grew with the time and voice. Soft poetry
did rhyme
With graceful flowing body lines her dancing always was
in time.

In every person's face did rise a smile upon their meeting
And never was their heart so full upon this special greeting

And no one from the world around would leave her
without thinking
Of the happiness she brought to them
With her smile and eyes a twinkling.

They say that she from fairies came upon that autumn day
And she vanishes completely if it ever starts to rain.

And folk do come from miles around to see her just to cheer
their minds
And walk away without a care, no wicked thoughts can cling
to her.

And then, one day, her life was done she floated up towards
the sun.
With colours like the autumn leaves of reds and golds
Streaming it seems

Across the sky of autumn blue to cascade down, where? No
one knew
Around the parish it was heard was born again, this
autumn girl
That did not cry but smiled and laughed

A fairy's reborn epitaph.

SECOND CHANCE

Did you know I cared for you long before you knew me?
Did you know I loved you, too, yes, I did so truly?

I saw you loved another so there was no chance for me
I elected to stay silent and forever just be free.

And as the world turned silently nature took its course.
There came another chance for me to always be just yours.

Yet still I love you truly and care for you so much,
Though the years have took their toll and left us with some rust.

But we can shake it off a bit and polish up so bright
And walk beneath the silvery moon, wandering through the night.

And as the dawn is breaking on a more than perfect morn,
We'll kick the dew from off the grass while walking on the lawn.

And go inside for breakfast toast with marmalade and tea
And I will say I love you and I hope that you love me.

YESTERDAYS

Don't let your yesterdays
Spoil your tomorrows!

What has been and gone,
all the tears and sorrows,

Leave them all behind
and look forward to see

all the joy and laughter
To please you and me!

For you'll never change
What's already been done

So smile and accept all the
laughter and fun

That's around every corner
or just around the bend

So enjoy every minute
with your family and friends!

RUN BOTH WAYS

Highways and telephone lines they are both the same
They make it easy to excuse or sometimes to explain.
I call them often just to see if they are all right or may not be.
Their voice it lightens at my call. We chatter on about it all.

The ins and outs of life itself and how life's left them on the
shelf.
A visit they say would be nice, so I would go and see their eyes
alive and bright at this surprise.

We would talk long within the night about all things we may
or might
but soon it seems I have to go into the darkness, rain or snow.
I often wonder as I may that roads and phones they run both
ways.
But people in their busy life, so full of everything and strife,

Forget it takes but just one call to cheer you up and change it
all.
And so I feel in future days I'll say to them it runs both ways.

So don't forget to come or call for you just might have changed
it all.

GHOSTS

While little boys we heard the tales of ghostly things that
banged and wailed
and opened doors that had been locked, threw out the blankets
from their box,
and strewn around the landing be at morning there for all
to see.

It happens on November nights when everything is dark
and lights
have been extinguished hours ago and fires long lost their
friendly glow.
Then out would come those ghosts of old, tormented souls of
long ago,
and cast their spells and move around this human space,
without a sound.

With mischief made throughout the house which lay so still,
not even mouse would dare to make the smallest sound,
while these old souls silently about.

So one day this notion came into our heads, we'd play
this game
and spy upon those ghostly forms to see their deeds and quell
our qualms.

Onto the landing out we crept and emptied blankets from
their chests,
creeping within this wooden tomb to watch and wait within
the gloom.
Time was slow, the night was long and restlessness too
tired began
we drifted off into a sleep of restlessness and fits of dreams.

With ghostly forms, tormented souls and ghosts that chased us
through the halls,

and spirits that would burst alive from walls and floors with
intent eyes.

Within our tomb the night grew chill, one blanket saved
seemed not enough,
when, all at once, the lid was thrown, open wide with one
great groan,
A spectre stood in awful form before us both at early morn.
We gasped and looked into its eyes with gruffest voice we
were surprised.

"You boys have been long out of bed the ghosts have been and
gone", it said.
Then, realising our mistake, our father stood there while we
quaked,
For all along the landing locked doors were open wide,
With blankets strewn around the place and blanket chests
their lids agape.

And never did we take the chance to spy on ghosts for just
one glance
but left them to their eternal ways, perplexing humans with
their games.

IN ANOTHER LIFE

She sat there demurely, with her six score years and ten.
Add another twenty and a lifetime of content.
You would think her hands were only used for drinking wine
or tea,
With one finger raised so elegantly.
You're surely wrong! You see

Although she drips with elegance refined, with fancy clothes,
Her real life from long ago lays just where? No one knows.

For if you hear her conversation when she gets in the mood,
She will talk about her life long gone,
An existence much more crude.

Her family they were farmers and she had to help as well
To catch and clean the animals, regardless of the smell.

And soon became adapt at things that ladies never do,
Like catching sheep and herding cows and moving heaps of poo.

One day she reached that kind of age when girls they start
to bloom
And boys they start to notice and hang around the parlour room.

Her father said get off to bed, tomorrow make an early rise,
For off to market we will go, a wicked glint within his eyes.

He took her off to market and stood her by the pen
Which held so many cattle which he hoped to sell.

The only orders that he gave were to lean upon the rails
And study all his cows in there, from their heads to tails.

And, as the months went by, she often wondered why she came
Every week to market to play this silly game.

And so she asked her father what all this was about
And got a wink and smile and nudge as he pointed out

That his daughter was the prettiest thing this market's ever seen,
And, instead of looking at other pens, men are always watching
mine.

For the filly that's enchanting them makes sure every time
That I sell my pen of cattle, for they say that love is blind.